Rocking in OXFORD

A Personal History of the 1960s and 1970s Music Scene

Published by
Chris Andrews Publications Ltd
15 Curtis Yard
North Hinksey Lane
Oxford
OX2 0LX
Tel +44(0)1865 723404
Web: www.cap-ox.co.uk

ISBN 978 1 906725 20 4

First published 2009
© Text: Trevor Hayward
© Pictures: The bands themselves; Chris Andrews;
Arthur Titterington; Newsquest Oxford (*Oxford Mail*
and *Oxford Times*); Alamy; Morgue File; author's
pictures p77 by Haynes. Every effort has been made
to contact sources and copyright holders. In the
event of any errors or omissions, the publishers
will be happy to make corrections in subsequent
editions
© This design and production: Chris Andrews
Publications Ltd

Design: Mike Brain

Printed by leachprint

TO
DAVINA AND
TREV

KEEP

Rocking
in OXFORD

A Personal History of the 1960s
and 1970s Music Scene

Trevor Hayward

GOOD HEALTH

TREV

BOOKLAUNCH
OCT 3rd 2009

Chris Andrews Publications Limited

To my late friend Shaun Ditchburn who started me on the roller coaster ride that is live rock music. It's all your fault mate, and I thank you dearly for it.

Contents

ON THE STAGE ONE WEEK ONLY

NEW THEATRE

Phone: **OXFORD** 44544/5

Proprietors: THE OXFORD THEATRE CO. LTD.   Managing Director: STANLEY C. DORRILL, M.B.E.
Director and General Manager: JOHN DORRILL

WEEK COMMENCING MONDAY, 7TH DECEMBER, 1964

TWICE NIGHTLY 5.50 AND 8.20

ARTHUR HOWES presents

FROM THE U.S.A.

GENE PITNEY

The Dynamic   KINKS

MONDAY TO FRIDAY ONLY

OXFORD'S OWN

FALLING LEAVES

DAILEY
AND
WAYNE

MIKE COTTON SOUND

VAL McCALLUM

THE POETS

HIT RECORDERS OF NOW WE'RE THRU'

SATURDAY ONLY

BOBBY SHAFTO
WITH THE ROOFRAISERS

ELECTRIC MODERN PRINTING CO. LTD., MANCHESTER 4

ST. JOHN AMBULANCE BRIGADE
COUNTY OF OXFORD

APPEAL YEAR 1967

BLENHEIM PARK, WOODSTOCK

By kind permission of His Grace the Duke of Marlborough & the Rt. Hon. The Marquis of Blandford.

SUNDAY, JULY 23rd,
From 4 p.m. - 6 p.m.
Doors open 2.30 p.m.

GRAND

POP CONCERT

Adrian Hopkins presents, on behalf of the Appeal

MANFRED MANN
JEFF BECK
P. P. ARNOLD with her NICE
SIMON DUPREE & THE BIG SOUND
PLUS LOCAL GROUPS

Tickets 10/- per person, obtainable from Mrs. P. C. Stett,
St. John Ambulance Brigade County H.Q., 14 Church Street,
St. Ebbe's, Oxford.   S.A.E. please.

Printed by OLIVER & SON (Oxford) LTD.

TREV
Profile (The Start)

1969, John Mason Grammar School, Abingdon. My late friend Shaun Ditchburn decided to form a rock band (he had his own bass guitar and we were impressed!) and asked me to play drums. Now, I had always fancied myself as a guitarist but there were too many guitarists and no drummers so I agreed even though there was a severe lack of Hayward Drum Kit!

Help was on hand in the shape of my gorgeous girlfriend, Sandie Webb, who told me there was a kit at Southmoor Village Hall and they wanted to sell it for £25.

The next day I rushed across there, my young mind full of images of sparkling drums and shiny cymbals. From the inside of a small dusty cupboard, bits of rusty ironmongery and dented cymbals were introduced to me along with the drums which were contained in two Hessian sacks. I think they were last played on VE night. I knocked the price down to £19 and took them home, much to the consternation of the neighbours.

After a few rehearsals we were unleashed on an unsuspecting public at an end of term dance at school. I can still remember taking the stage to the barrage of noise that only 300 schoolchildren can make.

We played four songs twice and finished with an Edgar Broughton Band number with a chorus of "kill the pigs" that got us promptly evicted from the stage.

So began the young Hayward's music career which would span 41 years and 25 bands. I loved the music then and still do, it's been great fun.

TREV

Introduction

Oxford – the very name conjures images. Dreaming spires, weatherbeaten colleges, ageing dons discussing the nature of existence, students on their bicycles … Oxford is home to the oldest University in the English-speaking world and its contributions cannot easily be ignored. From philosophy to physics, medicine to metallurgy, and classics to chemistry, the University is world renowned. The town is not, however, only a home to academe. In recent history William Morris developed car manufacturing and created an industrial counterpart to the old University City. Car manufacturing still continues in the city, but today high technology firms have sprung up in business parks on the edge of the city. And music … Oxford is famous for its music. New College Choir, Carols from Magdalen College, Haydn's Oxford symphony (first performed in the Sheldonian Theatre here), Holywell Music Room, and a whole host of other aspects of the classical tradition. But when one thinks of popular music one does not think immediately of Oxford. But maybe one should!

CARFAX ASSEMBLY ROOMS

1963

Saturday, Feb. 16, 8–11.45 p.m.

The Sensational Recording Stars—

THE BEATLES

(please, please me)

PLUS THE MADISONS

Advance tickets (limited) 6/-, Russell Acotts,
High Street

CHAPTER 1
The Beatles in Oxford

Think of the Sixties. The biggest thing to hit the music scene at the time had to be The Beatles. Love them or hate them, just about everyone had heard of them, and they didn't ignore Oxford and Oxfordshire. Indeed they came to this part of the world three times, and the Oxford reserve melted away. They made an enormous impact, and even got an invite to dine at an Oxford College.

The first visit on February 16, 1963 brought them to the legendary Carfax Assembly rooms, sited at number 63 Cornmarket where the HSBC cashpoint hall now stands. Just back from playing Hamburg, the Fab Four turned up early in the afternoon for a sound check, as did local band The Madisons.

Lead guitarist of the Madisons Will Jarvis recalls the afternoon: 'We arrived in the afternoon and ended up rehearsing with them. Paul on the piano playing old Chuck Berry numbers. They were really nice lads and after the sound check we decided to go for a Chinese meal in Ship Street before the gig and asked them along. John and Paul came along but we didn't see Ringo and George until the evening. That night after playing our set, we stayed and watched them rather than go to The Crown pub around the corner, which was normal! It was obvious to us that they were something special and the packed audience had to be kept away from the stage with an arrangement of tables and chairs, something we had never seen before.'

That week, their second record 'Please Please Me' was at number 3 and the previous week 'Love Love Me Do' had got to number 27. The following week 'Please Please Me' got to number 2, and their following three singles 'From Me to You', 'She Loves You' and 'I Want to Hold Your Hand' got to number one. The tickets for the gig cost six shillings! (30p).

The Beatles' second appearance in Oxfordshire was on the outskirts of the pleasant market town of Witney. It was November 1, 1963. The famous four had just returned from playing in Sweden. After being greeted by hordes of fans at Heathrow they were on their way to appear at Cheltenham. Feeling tired and hungry their black Austin Princess came to halt outside the Windrush pub on the A40. Oxford Mail photographer Arthur Tithering takes up the story:

The Beatles at the Windrush near Witney.

'My office was alerted to The Beatles by the staff of the Windrush. It was decided that we should have a photograph of them so I was dispatched to do so. When I arrived The Beatles were just leaving. I asked their road manager if I could take a few shots. Initially he was cautious saying that the lads were tired and needed to get onto Cheltenham, but he eventually agreed.'

The famous photograph now hangs in the foyer of the Windrush. As an example of the fame and popularity of the group at the time, when word reached the local school, Wood Green, that the Beatles had just visited the local pub, the pupils rushed up to the Windrush car park to pick up bits of gravel that the Beatles car had run over. Who needs moon-rock?

The third time the mop tops came this way was in March 1964. They were invited to dine at Brasenose College by the then

23-year-old Jeffrey Archer who was fundraising for Oxfam and thought the publicity would be helpful. A special Beatles train was supposed to stop at Didcot, and then the boys would be driven to Oxford. Unfortunately, word had got out and hordes of local schoolgirls had crowded on to the platform. The Beatles eventually got off the train at Cholsey, leaving a throng of adoring girls screaming 'We want The Beatles' for more

than two hours! One particularly grumpy rail worker threw a bucket of water over them … but this only made them chant louder. Later the Principal of Brasenose College, Sir Noel Hall, said they were four exceptionally agreeable young men. After the meal The Beatles went across the High to the exclusive Vincent's Club, a private club for University students who have gained a Blue in sports. More pictures were taken, with young Jeffrey Archer in the background, and to this day these photos hang in the bar alongside many awards for sporting triumphs.

After appearing in Oxford The Beatles toured the USA. In April 1964 they held the top five places on the Billboard Singles Chart – a feat never to be repeated! The British invasion had begun. The American people fell in love with our lads and who could blame them!

CHAPTER 2
In Oxford Before they were Famous

In 1963, a year before they were famous, The Rolling Stones accepted a booking at Magdalen College for the princely sum of £100. A year later, in June 1964, they had to cut short a tour of America to return to play the gig. The cost of the flight was £1,500 but they were contracted and could not get out of this particular obligation. It was Magdalen College's Commemoration Ball and by now the Stones could have been expected to be paid somewhere in the region of £500. One of the organisers of the Ball said at the time 'it's the bargain of the year,' a sentiment no doubt also held by Mick Jagger and his colleagues.

One of the other acts appearing were Oxford's very own Falling Leaves. In fact Bill Wyman, the bass player in the Stones, used one of their amplifiers because of a

The Rolling Stones at Magdalen College, 1964.

malfunction with his own equipment. This was not the only time the Stones played Oxford before hitting the big time.

On January 4, 1964 a young Simon Edens was backstage at Oxford Town Hall. He says of that night: 'My father, Les Edens, was at the time responsible for booking bands and groups at the Town Hall, so I quite often used to get back stage. I'd seen Brian Poole and the Tremeloes, The Searchers, The Swinging Blue Jeans and P.J. Proby. The night of the fourth stands out for me. I can remember a tatty old white van pulling up outside the hall and lots of lads getting out. They had very long hair for the time and were rushing around a lot. After they had set up their gear I went back stage to say hello. A very skinny man came up to me and asked if I had a spare cigarette. It was Mick Jagger, and no, I never got one back! Perhaps I should drop him a line.'

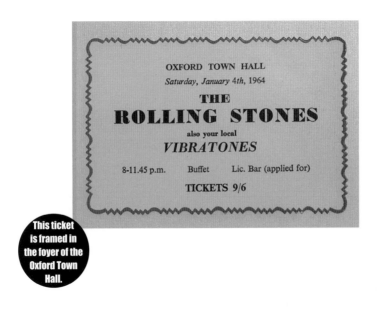

OXFORD TOWN HALL
Saturday, January 4th, 1964
THE
ROLLING STONES
also your local
VIBRATONES

8-11.45 p.m.   Buffet   Lic. Bar (applied for)

TICKETS 9/6

This ticket is framed in the foyer of the Oxford Town Hall.

Status Quo

Elms Court, Botley, on the edge of Oxford City is an area of suburban housing and small businesses. No dreaming spires here, but still it could, on occasion, pull in the crowds. In the late Sixties it was on the main English gig circuit, although not all the acts were exactly chart topping. On Sunday 9th June, 1968 Status Quo (formerly known as Traffic Jam) were booked to appear. These days the Quo, as they are known, can sell out just about any venue in minutes, but back in the late Sixties they struggled to fill the venue.

Jeff Samways ticket signed by The Quo.

Front of ticket, note number 002 – who had no 001?

Music fan Jeff Samways of Abingdon, who went a long way to increase the audience that night, takes up the story: 'I hired a small coach and took along about 15 of my friends from Fitzharrys School. It was a good night. Status Quo were in flash clothes, yellow and red with bell-bottom trousers.' The attendance that night was a little over 30 people. After the gig the band signed the back of Mr Samways ticket, which he has kept to this day. The cost of entrance was 10 shillings (50p).

Quo ticket 2008 ... price now £31.50

Pink Floyd at the Stage Club

In May 1967 a relatively unknown group appeared at the Stage Club above George Street in central Oxford. They would go on to change the visual appeal of pop music around not only Oxford, but the entire world. Nick Mason, Rick White, Roger Waters and Syd Barrett comprised a group known then as The Pink Floyd. What was unique about this group was they travelled with their own dedicated light show rather than depend on theatre spotlights, and for the time the visual spectacular they put on was awe inspiring. Light mosaics were beamed on to the walls of the venue. The patterns delighted audiences and were a product of light being projected through oil filled gel filters, a technology now long gone, but revolutionary at the time. The infinite colours and shapes delighted the audience, who were used to simply seeing bands perform without such a light show. Ultra-violet lighting was used at the time, revealing fluorescent teeth, hair and dandruff!

As music fan Les Hallett recalls: 'I used to go to the Stage Club when they had a band on. It was a good place to go because it had a late license! I was 20 in 1967 and had already seen Joe Cocker and the Grease Band there. On this particular night it was Pink Floyd. I had heard of them before, 'See Emily Play' had just been released, but to be honest that night I went because all my friends were there. I can remember all the lights and oil slides being projected on the band and on the walls. The music was very futuristic and loud! It was a different type than I had been used to: I was into the Blues and R & B, like a lot of others of my age, and at the time I was not sure if I liked it. That first impression remains because I am still not sure if I like Pink Floyd, but the night was unusual and enjoyable.'

In an interview at that show with local journalist Anthony Wood the group were quoted as saying they were influenced by The Beatles – 'The only group we really admire. We are not psychedelic and we don't take LSD.' Makes you wonder what they did take to record songs about scarecrows, bicycles and cooking breakfast. I'll have some… The band gained the name 'Pink Floyd' from two Georgia blues men Pink Anderson and Floyd Council, as their initial inspiration, some suggest, came from the Blues. Perhaps, a far cry from what they were to become.

Bowie At The Town Hall

He had been at the top of the charts in 1969 with 'Space Oddity', a novelty record featuring a Rolf Harris stylophone but disappeared off the musical radar for the next three years. In June 1972 on his first tour of England he appeared at the Oxford Town Hall. Bowie was in his Ziggy Stardust days and just before the release of his next single 'Starman', which was to catapult him into mega-stardom. The entire band were dressed in shiny clothes that looked like that lagging of a water tank. Bowie fan Alicia Phillips remarked: 'I'd heard of Bowie from Discos and the *Melody Maker*. I thought he was different and fresh, and had what today would be called the 'X' factor! Everything about him appealed to me – his music, his dress and his hair. I think I went to Russell Acott on the High in my lunch hour to buy the tickets, and was ecstatic when I purchased them for me and my friend. I can remember going to the gig in velvet 'loon' pants and platform heels. The gig was a concert but quite a few of the girls got up and decided to dance at the front. I wanted to get a better view and went up to the balcony – we were so close to him we seemed like we could touch him. I loved the gig and can remember it to this day and later when he went to the top of the charts with 'Starman' we gloated we had tickets to see him beforehand. Although it was great that night they were very few people there, maybe about two hundred, but we enjoyed it immensely and since then I've always been a fan.'

David Bowie and Mick Ronson at the Town Hall.

The Brick Company and Pytheon Productions present

IN CONCERT

WISHBONE ASH
RENAISSANCE
STACKRIDGE

ON TOUR IN JUNE
DETAILS OVER LEAF

Oxford Town Hall.

CHAPTER 3
Venues Past and Present

Standing at the top of St Aldates, a major road leading from the south into Oxford city, the Town Hall sits quiet and sedate like a becalmed ocean liner watching the world go by. This grand old lady of municipal buildings was once a lot more flighty than she is now. To many people in Oxford, she's the centre of local government, to others a place of tea dances and record and CD sales (once a month, first weekend on a Saturday) but to teenagers back in the Sixties she was musical Valhalla. The New Theatre may have been the bigger venue, but the Town Hall was the place for up and coming groups to play.

Local musician Mick Harris told me what it was like to play at the Town Hall in the early Sixties. "I was in a band called the Electrons and we played there probably 15 or 16 times. In that era they were always dances. We were quite often the support band to some of the major acts that performed. One that springs to mind was Screaming Lord Sutch and The Savages and he was a total nightmare, rushing across the stage with a prop knife shouting at the top of his voice! We also supported Marty Wilde, Joe Brown and the Bruvvers, Cliff Richard and the Drifters, just when their song 'Move it' was getting to No 1. The Town Hall was always packed with lots of teenage girls who always screamed. Tickets at the time were around five shillings (25p). It was great to play there, the biggest dance venue in Oxford and everyone went there."

At the young age of 68, Mick is still playing in a group called Move It, still performing rock and roll in front of the dancers of Oxford. Good luck to him.

The audience would then rush through the creaky wooden doors at the front and up the elegant and impressive Victorian stone staircase, full of anticipation, through another set of doors and into the wonderful Victorian auditorium with its high ornate ceiling and balcony. On gig nights it would be alive with the buzz of people waiting for the next potential chart-topping act. In the Seventies some of the acts that appeared there were T Rex, Free, Coliseum, David Bowie, Wishbone Ash and the wonderful Carole Grimes.

I saw T-Rex there when they were touring under their original name, Tyrannosaurus Rex. It was an acoustic set. Young Marc Bolan, long hair, and a 12-string acoustic guitar. The group was a duo at the time and a young gentleman called Steve Peregrine-Took provided the percussion. I remember him doing a 10-minute solo on one conga drum! You could do things like that in the early Seventies! I'd like to see the good people at MTV shoot a video of that and get it to look interesting. A bit like a slide show of different sides of a billiard ball. But they were pioneering days.

I remember going to the Town Hall a lot in the early Seventies. It was **the** place to see up and coming bands. There were seats, but only one ticket price, so it was a free-for-all to get to the front. If you were really fleet of foot you went upstairs to the balcony where you were nearly on the stage! Most of the audiences at the time seemed to be held together with denim and hair, not unlike myself, and there was always someone shouting for his mate "Wally".

The Town Hall also played its part in the formation of the Sixties first 'super group'. In 1966 Eric Clapton was at the Town Hall playing with John Mayall's Blues Breakers group. Ginger Baker came along to watch. At the time he was playing with the Graham Bond Organisation along with Jack Bruce. Ginger offered Eric a lift back to London after the gig and proposed he and Eric should form a band. The guitarist agreed as long as Jack played with them. Baker thought long and hard because he and Jack had never got along terribly well, but he eventually decided to go along with the idea. So from a meeting at Oxford Town Hall the famous Sixties super group Cream was formed.

Sadly, in the mid Seventies, the decision was taken to stop live bands playing at the venue, the reason given being that the volume of the groups had grown significantly over the years and there was a real danger of the magnificent Victorian plasterwork falling on the heads of the audience. Talk about bringing the house down!

The problem has now been rectified, and happily the Town Hall is now available for bookings, although it has never regained its popularity with touring groups, the New Theatre now taking preference.

Elms Court, Botley

Built in 1964 the Elms Court Ballroom was typical of the buildings of the time, bricks, concrete and square in design, its outside had very little architectural merit. It was, however, a top nightspot in Oxford for the best part of 20 years. Known also as Sands Discothèque and at a later date Blades Nightclub during its time, it was a cross between disco and live music. Many well known groups of the time played here including The Casuals, Amen Corner, Simon Dupree, P.P. Arnold, The Move and The Tremeloes. There was also an early showing of the Rocky Horror Show.

The venue was well supported during the Sixties and early Seventies, but by the Eighties it went into something of a decline. Touring artists shunned the venue, and instead top acts opted for the larger and more profitable New Theatre in the city centre. The owners of the site, seeing profits fall, finally closed the doors in 1994 and the building was demolished in the same year. A library, a bank and offices now occupy the space in a building that is perhaps even less prepossessing than what went before.

The last time I was there the group performing was called Shag Connors and The Carrot Crunchers. A fine band no doubt – chickens (really, they had them!) and all, but not, as time has indicated, obvious chart-toppers. Really, there were chickens…!

SANDS

ELMS DISCOTHEQUE BOTLEY
COURT OXFORD

OPENING GALA NIGHT

THURSDAY 12 JUNE

FROM RADIO 1 THE FABULOUS

MIKE RAVEN

SHOW

LONDON'S TOP **GO GO** GIRLS

OTHER TOP D.J.s

8 – MIDNIGHT

FULLY LICENSED BAR   PRIZES !

ADMISSION
6/-

Diane Gibbs told me what it was like to go to Elms Court.

'I was 15 in September 1968. Elms Court had opened earlier in that summer. As our parents thought we were too young to be allowed to go in, my friends and I used to hang around outside the building on the evenings that groups like The Herd and Love Affair were appearing, in the hope that we would catch a glimpse of them as they went in – not that we were ever lucky!

'Then we found that Amen Corner were booked to appear that Christmas! Along with the two groups as mentioned before, they were one of the "boy bands" of that period and had recently had a No 1 hit with Bend Me Shape Me. As I was 15 by then, my parents said they would allow me to go, so I planned to go along with several friends, Sue, Jill, Alicia, Janice and some others.

'We got our tickets, which cost 20 shillings (£1) each, from Russell Acott Music Shop in the High Street (I think). I had a Saturday job in a greengrocers, which gave me the money for my ticket.

'Amen Corner were appearing on Saturday 21 December 1968. I didn't know what to wear so I borrowed some clothes from a school friend. I can remember them clearly – black maxi culottes and a white, high necked, long sleeved Victorian style blouse. My mother thought I looked dreadful, but I was quite happy – I liked to look different and at this time, most girls were still wearing mini skirts so I probably stood out a bit!

'The dance hall was packed with lots of other people we knew from Bretts ("Tickets" as the under 18 dance nights were known) and the local Botley youth club, which was actually in Elms Court basement. We were too young to drink alcohol, but were happy just to be there dancing.

'After the support acts, Ultra Sounds and Zachary Boot, we were ready for Amen Corner! They played all their hits and some other songs too. I was most thrilled because I managed to touch Andy's (Fairweather-Low) hand! It made my night! This was my first time at a live gig and I thought it was a fantastic night, right from the start around eight until it ended at midnight. I still have my ticket as a souvenir.'

The Forum

On the left hand side of the High Street heading towards St Clements there is a rather unwelcoming alleyway located between No 50 – Bajan Blue – and No 51 – Roses Tea Rooms. This used to be the entrance to The Forum, a very popular dance hall in the late Fifties and early Sixties.

Janet Fisher, a teenager at the time and a regular at The Forum told me what it was like to go there.

'I was 16 when my friends and I first went to The Forum, we went there for the dancing. We would go there most weekends with our glad rags on, which in those days used to be a very full skirt, white high-heeled shoes and a blouse. We would meet at Lyons Tea Rooms on the corner of Carfax, do our hair and make-up, and then off to The Forum. It was two shillings (10p) to get in and the highlight of the night was to sit and have a cup of coffee – all very trendy and grown up at the time. One night after performing, Long John Baldry joined us for a drink (no milk and three sugars) and told us of his plans for the future. We also saw Status Quo there; the tickets were five shillings (25p). They played there again but the tickets had gone up and we couldn't afford them. The Forum became quite famous I remember meeting people who had travelled from Swindon to be there.'

Larry Redding, a young drummer at the time, explained what it was like to appear there.

'In 1964 and 1965 I was in a band called The Falling Leaves and we played there quite often. The Forum was putting on a Trad Jazz night once a week. We were a rhythm and blues band but they wanted us as a warm-up act. One of the biggest jazz acts we supported was Acker Bilk. The dance hall was a fairly large place but quite bleak and Victorian. You walked down a passage from the High Street to a building which was in the Quad of the College. It was freestanding and quite like a small Town Hall. It was always packed and fun to play.'

As this book goes to print, Larry is in his 52nd year of drumming – good for him!! It makes my 41 years look like a novice.

The Forum continued to hold dances until June 1965 when on the 16th of that month, the last entertainment was held there. In July of that year it was demolished and work started on accommodation for St Edmund Hall, who owned the site.

The last word on The Forum goes to Janet Fisher. 'As the years went on The Forum became very popular and we used to have to get there about 6.30 to make sure we could get in. Until it shut it was the best place, the very best place to go in Oxford. Happy days!'

A great epitaph from a much-loved venue.

The Falling Leaves.

Carfax Assembly Rooms

Number 63 Cornmarket Street is the HSBC Bank's cash point hall. It has also been a shoe shop (Ravels) and a snack bar and cafeteria, but to many people from Oxford and the surrounding area this was the entrance to the Carfax Assembly Rooms. It was a top venue in Oxford from the mid-Fifties to the late Sixties, a place where young people from the city and county used to dance the night away to top local bands and touring national groups.

The Carfax Assembly Rooms in 1961

Rock concert solution may be foot step away

A SHOE shop which hides an old dance hall behind its smart city-centre frontage says it Street, which was in business until about 15 years ago.

The shoe shop's own-

Courtesy of Oxford Mail /Oxford Times (Newsquest Oxford)

The building was owned by the Oxford and District Co-op (a large chain store) and had several different club nights, Monday was the University Club night, Tuesday was the Perdido Club with their modern jazz, and Wednesday was the trad jazz night with Acker Bilk turning up to play in 1959. At weekends the Ballroom, later to be called the Orchid Rooms, had mainly pop groups and dances with an occasional talent contest. The revellers entered through the front via the cafe and up a wide staircase into the upstairs dance hall. The cafe also had a stage and by night doubled as another dance hall. You might think that sprung dance floors are a product of our modern world but even then this technology was in use at this venue, much to the delight of the energetic 'jivers'. It had a capacity of around 700, a large venue in a small provincial town for the Fifties. At that time the craze for 'jiving' and 'jitterbugging' caused a bit of problem of busy dance nights. Eddie Turton, manager of the Assembly Rooms, was bemused and, not a man to mix his words, exclaimed 'they are decadent and primitive', and local dance band leader Stan Rogers was inclined to agree, describing them as a curse on ballroom dancing. It is hard to imagine what they would make of a modern rave, but perhaps even harder to imagine their reaction today to find that the place is a bank.

Margaret Messenger, a cheery young reveller, recalls those heady days: 'I used to go to the Assembly Rooms in the Fifties and Sixties, quite often with my boyfriend. At the time there was a limited amount of opportunity for doing the dances we both loved – the jive and the jitterbug. On one particularly packed and exciting evening we went along to dance to Stan Rogers and his band. It was a great night – jitterbugging was allowed unless it was a nuisance to other dancers. These days if you see the dance on TV, the girls have flat shoes and tights and ankle socks, but in the late Fifties it was high heels and stocking and suspenders. We were really enjoying ourselves when we went for a particular move which entailed my legs around his waist. I then had a tap on the shoulder from someone who we later found out was the floor manager and he said you have to stop dancing because you are causing a disturbance! Apparently a glance of stocking tops and knickers was considered at the time extremely shocking. We carried on dancing in the traditional way but ended up going home early. Embarrassed? Not me, I'd been a ballet dancer for a while and the sight of a naked thigh in that form was normal, but I never did wear stockings again.'

The Assembly Rooms finally shut their doors in 1966. A sad day for thousands of people throughout Oxfordshire who had seen the Beatles play there and had waltzed and jived with future spouses. The Ballroom remained hidden to the outside world for over a decade, its entrance hall no longer tempting late night revellers but instead by day a shoe shop. In 1981, however, its future seemed more promising. Richard Branson owner of the Virgin Group, and a local Oxford man, proposed to spend £250,000 to bring this historic venue back to life. He proposed a facelift to the site and, perhaps unsurprisingly, one of his record stores to replace the shoe shop. Eventually these plans fell on stony ground due to modern fire regulations that demanded alterations that proved unfeasible.

The Stage Club

Situated on the corner of George Street and Victoria Court above what is now 'Bella Italia' was the Stage Club. It almost literally rose from the ashes of the Clarendon Restaurant that had burnt down in 1966. Sitting amid the wreckage of his restaurant, Thomas Hook, the owner, put into action a plan that had been in his mind for a while – to open a club where people could get a meal and cheap drink after a show at the New Theatre opposite. Opening in January 1967, the club housed an up to the minute 'discothèque', a bar with a late licence (rare for the 60s) and was host to the occasional group.

Steve Theobald remembers it well: 'I started going to the Stage Club in 1971. At the time they were doing the odd meal to get the late licence but most of the time I went for the discos. After a couple of beers in the city pubs we would head for George Street, cross the road to Victoria Court by the theatre, and climb up the two flights of steps to the club. We generally went there after 10:30, which was closing time in pubs back then. So, a hot dog was the order of the day to keep the club legal. The first floor of the Stage was a disco with the occasional group, whereas the second floor was more of a 'chill out' area. The club was often well attended, it was a membership only club, but luckily because of its split level layout not always packed. I remember in 1972 they introduced a 10p a shot night on Fridays and that seemed to increase the membership a lot!' Cheap drink has always been popular… 'It was at the Stage Club that my best friend and I met our future wives on the same night, so the 10p a shot has a lot to answer for! The club shut in 1974 and like the majority of my friends from back then we started going down the Corn Dolly in Frewin Court, off Cornmarket Street, which had just opened and had live bands pretty much every night.'

The Corn Dolly

Tucked away in Frewin Court, a small and apparently insignificant alleyway off Cornmarket Street is a bar now called The Cellar. As The Corn Dolly It opened in the early Seventies and soon became a mecca for young people in Oxford who wanted to see and hear live music. With its policy of having acts on every night, and on weekends at mid-day, it soon established itself as **the** live music venue in Oxford. Bands from all over the country queued up to perform there and in its later years it was on the English gig circuit, its weekly programme advertised in the *NME* and *Melody Maker*.

Local musicians Nigel Lawrence and Julian Denson recall the venue: 'We played there in various groups in the Seventies and early Eighties and the Dolly was always a challenge. Carrying all of the gear down the steep steps was a tiring start to begin with, and then setting up was always cramped, the stage was no more than some wooden planks on beer crates, with a carpet on top, so we were only a few inches above the audience. Once set up we had a beer at the bar, or would go next door to the Crown. The Dolly was always busy and by the time we were on you could hardly move. The bar was always crushed, and people would be standing in the centre of the room with their beers. If you got a seat in one of the alcoves that was a triumph! Sometimes the only place to be was on the stage, and we always had a crate of beer with us. As the night wore on it became even more crowded and with the heat the walls would run with condensation. It was very rare to get any applause from the audience for a couple reasons: to begin with most of the audience played in bands and consequently regarded themselves as too cool to clap the competition, and also if you were standing in the middle of the room with your

Frewin Court, showing The Cellar bar – formerly The Corn Dolly .

The author letting them know who's boss at The Dolly, circa 1978.

drink in one hand clapping is not a wise move. That being said, it was always good to play there and if you did get some applause you knew you had done a good job.'

Writing this reminds me that one of the landlords had a huge Great Dane dog. During setting up and sound checks he was always a bit too friendly, but as soon as the gig proper started he'd be up the stairs and out of the pub… he'd go off to The Crown for a quiet time, and then return at closing time to see you off the premises.

The Jericho Tavern

In 1979 I formed a wonderful, raucous rock bank called Mongrel. The name I thought summed up the personnel, all of us having been around a bit, playing in lots of different bands. We were in your face rock and took no prisoners. The audience might not have liked us but couldn't ignore us. The worst thing on stage is to play your best set only to hear the click of dominoes going down. I was looking for gigs for the band at the time and as luck would have it went to a friend's birthday party at the Jericho. It had recently stopped being a Berni Inn and had a large function room upstairs where the restaurant had been. Always on the look-out at the time for new venues, the Hayward brain sprang into action and I approached the then landlord Colin Taylor. I asked him if I could put Mongrel on and he agreed for the following Saturday. We would be printing the posters, tickets and put someone on the door.

The following week we played a couple of gigs and this resulted in us selling about 75 tickets for the Tavern, must of which were to a load of bikers from Bicester – they really liked rock music.

On the Saturday morning of the gig I received a phone call from Colin saying he had decided to cancel. When I asked him why, he said that the concert had not sold very well. I told him the amount of tickets we had sold and where they were coming from. He asked if there might be any trouble? I said I wasn't sure but if I'd have travelled from Bicester I might be a bit miffed, to say the least! The gig was back on and the evening was excellent. Everyone enjoyed it and after that we had a gig there once every month.

Through the Eighties, the Jericho's popularity grew and grew its gig listings appearing in the national papers, *NME* and *Melody Maker* and with local bands like Ride, Radiohead and Supergrass playing there, nationally it became the centre of what is now called OX POP.

To this day the Tavern still provides an extremely good venue for up-and- coming bands to ply their trade and the good news is, at the time of printing, its future seems assured.

I have fond memories of playing the Jericho. One was manhandling huge speakers up a very narrow staircase at the back that has a 180-degree bend in it! The other is the strange layout of the upstairs room when we played there. It was split into two areas, one with the bar and seating in it the other with the 'stage' and dance area. In between was a wall with a small archway in it! It was not unusual to hear applause and whistles from the large crowd but not actually see them! This was unlike some other gigs in Oxford I'd played when you could see the audience but not hear the applause!!

The Jericho Tavern, still there only somewhat changed from the 70s!

Russell Acott

Situated directly opposite The Mitre on the High (the place incidentally where much of this book was written), what is now a wine bar called All Bar One used to be a wonderful music shop by the name of Russell Acott. In fact, the name is still in the chequered tiles in the entrance. It was a veritable rabbit warren of a shop, the grand Steinway pianos in the basement, on the ground floor everything from kazoos to violins and upstairs a record department (those round black things … you must remember them!) whose staff had a knowledge of all things music that was superhuman!

Come with me on a typical Saturday afternoon in Oxford for young musicians like myself in the Seventies. The day generally started with meeting other like minded individuals at the Corn Dolly. Down the stairs we would go and spend the next couple of hours getting our rib cages vibrated and our hair rearranged by the sonic assault of one of many very good local bands that played there on a Saturday dinner time.

At 2.30 the bar shut (good for your liver, the Seventies, honest). There was then a mass exodus up the stairs and into the Wimpy burger bar on Cornmarket (waitress service, would you believe). After taking in the nutrients necessary for the next few hours off we would go down the High Street to Russell Acott armed only with two cans of lager in one pocket and 20 Number Six in the other (Number Six were a cigarette of such minute proportions that if you lit one in a breeze you were lucky to get more than one puff on it before it had smoked itself – still they were cheap (20p for 20, god how that ages me).

Once inside the door it was a quick look at the postcards – 'Drummer wanted for rock band and must play like Carl Palmer', 'New Hendrix required for folk band', 'Road Manager needed for working group, must have own van and licence or someone else's' – that type of thing. There then followed the 'faffing around' period where we all drooled over instruments that were to totally out of our price range but the guitarists would always try them out. We drummers were not allowed to hit drums so we would spend the next minutes listening to the opening chords of Deep Purple's 'Smoke on the Water' emanating from the latest Fender or Gibson (it still makes me cringe now). Upstairs now to the sanctuary of the record department, picking out a few LPs (long playing records) by the likes of King Crimson or Led Zeppelin. We would approach our friend Teresa for a listening booth. These were rooms you could easily fit eight or 10 people and there we would while away the time listening, drinking and smoking (yes you could smoke in shops in those innocent days!).

Acott's was that type of easy going place, full of classical musicians looking for sheet music, rock musicians looking for a job, hippies looking for the point of it all, and the occasional celebrity. I met Steve Winwood in there one day and after a quick chat he said we should meet when my band were playing. True to form, star talking to a lesser mortal, I never saw him again!

Russell Acott shut its High Street shop in 1999 after a mere 188 years of trading and moved to a warehouse in the suburbs.

I tried to play the bagpipes there once, honest. There wasn't too much melody but a few local cats threw themselves under the nearest station bus! Shame.

Whites Bar

OK my friends, I know that Whites Bar was not really a music venue (although I do remember the fabulous Steamroller playing there) but it did play a really important part in the music scene of Oxford in the Seventies and no book about this subject would be complete without.

Situated on the top of the High almost on Carfax in a premises now called Jigsaw – a fashion store – it was **the** place to go in the early Seventies.

Jigsaw Fashion shop used to be Whites Bar, Oh what nights we had!!

Whites had a reputation of being a rough place. This came from the times when the American servicemen from the US Air Force base at Upper Heyford used to use the upstairs lounge bar. The local lads occasionally used to take offence at these fine young gentlemen chatting up the local ladies. Physical discussion erupted quite often; it was a place my father said was quite rowdy so of course I went, well wouldn't you at 17?!

As you went in, the room stretched out before you. Whites wasn't very wide but it was long and so was the bar. All along the right-hand side ran some very comfortable leather seats, and above them the wall was plastered with LP sleeves from hundreds of different bands.

Right at the end of the room was the juke box, now this wasn't just **any** juke box; this was **the** juke box in Oxford.

I have no idea of the amplification that this wondrous piece of machinery had, but the down draught from the speakers in the ceiling had the same effect as a Sea King helicopter hovering about 10 feet above your head!

Kaftan coats were blow-dried, patchouli oil went everywhere and dandruff was a thing of the past! Such was the enjoyment of said machine that if you put a record selection on late Saturday night you just might be lucky enough to hear it at Sunday dinnertime.

Many different alien species congregated at Whites, all with the mutual love of beer (no wine then), and loud music. Bikers mixed with Mods, skinheads mixed with old Teddy Boys, and hippies talked to anyone who listened (generally other hippies, or the wallpaper!).

The Oranges and Lemons

Situated in St. Clements, The Oranges and Lemons (now called The Angel and Greyhound) was very important in the late Seventies and early Eighties in terms of the Punk and subsequent New Wave movement in Oxford.

In its earliest times of live music, it had a only juke box licence. This meant it could only have discos or duo's (two-piece groups) there. All this changed in 1977 when the stage was relocated to the front of the pub and double glazing was put in the front windows. An entertainment licence was granted unopposed. This opened the floodgates for groups of any size to perform there.

The young people of Oxford embraced New Wave with vigour and were soon to be seen wearing chains and pins, zips and rings, calf-length lace-up boots and erecting the amazing Mohican haircut.

Many of these anti-establishment teenagers got together to form bands. Some were good; others, let us say, were interesting! The order of the day when playing The Oranges and Lemons was image first, and then volume.

Now, being a rock musician for the best part of 40 years I am used to loud music, in fact, I quite enjoy it, but I have been there when the wine glasses on the top shelf have vibrated their way to the floor – now that's loud!

Of equal importance was the name of the band and in on-stage antics. Anyone who witnessed the totally off-the-wall performances of the wonderfully named Ken Liver Sausage and his band will never forget him hurtling across the stage, quite often a danger to himself!

The sublimely eccentric John Otway and wild Willy Barrett were regulars at the Oranges and always packed the place out.

I remember Split Screens, an exceptionally good New Wave band. And what about Handsome Dick and his Members! Honestly, you couldn't make it up.

RASHED INTO STOREFRONT

ro Pc saves a
ntleman's life

ceman became a
ved an elderly
crushed by a

ty in Magdalen
46 when he saw
ut of control and

the way as the
ment and
ow of Elliston &
t store known as
ls'.

quickly, there is
ould have died.
orted: "The truck
low of one of
wrooms.
of the Royal
stationary at the
Street.
nove off, it
al defect and
driver was
control and it
way and went
Glass was strewn

strians were
no-one was

SERVICE: Long service awards for staff at Elliston & Cavell and its sister company, William Baker and Co, at a Town Hall dinner in 1959 – left to right, Mr W T Woodley (37 years), Mr L H Foster (55), Miss F Butler (51), Mr P H Skelton (managing director), Mr E W Genman Hunter, Mr G Humphries (55), Mr H Scragg (56), with Mr H C Rose (chairman) seated. Below, an Elliston & Cavell delivery van

and a Mr Street.
Elliston soon had total control. In 1835, his chief clerk, John Caldecott

in 1951, there was no-one in the family to follow him.
Debenhams bought the business in

HEART-THROBS: The Falling Leaves, Oxford's answer to The Beatles

Great memories of Falling Leaves

I HAVE memories of the Oxford band, The Falling Leaves (*Memory Lane*, July 29 and August 5).

I was friends with Christine, the sister of Malcolm West, the group's bass player. We lived in the same road in Wolvercote.

We used to go on a Monday night to Blackbird Leys community centre where they played.

A coach was laid on for us fans to go to the TV studio for their performance in Ready Steady Win. Some people were chosen to dance and we were in the enthusiastic audience.

Another friend and I embroidered on to white T-shirts the words 'Falling Leaves' on the front and all their names on the back. We were very impressed with our handiwork.

I don't know what happened to the T-shirts, but I still have their record, She Loved to be Loved, which Christine and I purchased from Boots the Chemist as soon as it was released - we both worked there.

We were at the New Theatre to see them when they were brought in at the last minute to support Billy J Kramer in place of the sick Cilla Black in 1964.

Great memories.

SUE ZARECKY (nee Bayliss)
Kidlington

CHAPTER 4
Local Heroes

The Falling Leaves

They were formed in late 1963 by vocalist Rod Crisp and two members of The Madisons, mentioned earlier in this book as the support band to the Beatles when they played Oxford. The name, The Falling Leaves, was conjured up as something akin to The Rolling Stones, a group they all admired at the time.

Neil Robinson, keyboards for the Madisons and The Falling Leaves described the early days: 'Initially The Leaves played the type of music championed by Neil Sedaka we called the 'tra-la days', but as we grew we turned more and more to rhythm and blues, not unlike The Yardbirds, who were big at the time.'

Right from the start, The Falling Leaves were playing to large audiences in the City's three main venues – The Town Hall, The Forum and The Carfax Assembly Rooms. In the early Sixties there were no nightclubs or discos, so these venues were extremely popular with young people at the time when on Friday and Saturday nights dancing was the done thing.

A major breakthrough for the boys was when they secured a booking at Magdalen College Commemoration Ball in June 1964 supporting The Rolling Stones and legendary blues man John Lee Hooker, playing in a marquee, and alternating on stage all night with the Stones. This made them a reputation as a good support band, and stars of the time like Craig Douglas, Mike Berry and Manfred Mann booked the group.

The last gig mentioned was a concert rather than a dance – most unusual at time. The boys also played the New Theatre three times, supporting high-profile acts Billy J. Kramer, Cilla Black, and Gene Pitney. These UK tours had been organised by their then manager, Adrian Hopkins.

In mid 1964, The Falling Leaves turned professional. The last to do so was young guitarist Will Jarvis, whose father had advised him to finish his woodworking apprenticeship before going on the road.

Between 1964 and 1965 The Falling Leaves' schedule became more and more busy, starting off at two or three gigs a week rising to six or seven, touring all over England.

As Neil told me: 'The logistics weren't that good we could be in Newcastle one night and Portsmouth the next!

'Newcastle was a particularly good venue for us, we played with the Spencer Davis Group and Alan Price and The Animals. Another good thing to happen was the manager of the Concorde Club in Southampton came up to see us, his name was Carl Matheson and he signed us as resident band to replace Manfred Mann, who has achieved fame at the time and we were to replace them.

So in 1964 The Falling Leaves were resident band in two clubs almost 350 miles apart. Now that, dear reader, was being on the road in its truest sense.

Their largest gig was at the Fairfield Hall in Croydon, where they played alongside The Dave Clark Five and Millie Small of My Boy Lollipop fame. This was televised.

London beckoned and the group played the famous 100 club in Oxford Street, supporting The Graham Bond Organisation, whose bassist then was a young Jack Bruce, latterly of Cream. Neil told me: 'That night a strange thing happened, Jack touched the microphone with his lips and an electric shock surged through him, burning his fingers. He couldn't finish the show, so we had to go on and play again.'

The Falling Leaves played with Jack Bruce again at Merton College Commemoration Ball when he was with Cream.

They were signed with the Harold Davidson Agency, among whose acts were Gene Pitney, Billy J. Kramer, James Last, and even Frank Sinatra, quite heady stuff, I'm sure.

At the same time they secured a recording contract with the Parlaphone label, whose acts included The Beatles. They also had a track released on the Decca label. Other groups they played alongside were The Long John Baldry Band, whose second singer was a young Rod Stewart, and The Brian Auger Trinity with Julie Driscoll.

The Falling Leaves and their Parlophone record, 'She loves to be loved'.

PARLOPHONE

During the nine months between April and December 1964, The Falling Leaves played a total of 64 gigs and travelled nearly 7,000 miles in the days before a proper motorway network!! That's what you call a hard-working band.

Their last day playing together was in September 1966 at Smethwick Baths in the early evening and later at The Elbow Room, a businessmen's club in Birmingham. How typical for them – two gigs in one evening.

Eventually after shaving the British charts but not quite achieving the hit they so richly deserved, the lads decided to lower the curtain on The Falling Leaves. All the travelling and gigging almost every night taking its toll. So ends the story of The Falling Leaves, a nationally acclaimed Oxford Band, who I believe deserve the title Oxford's first supergroup.

Falling Leaves members: Will Jarvis, Neil Robinson, Rod Crisp, Larry Reddington, and Malcolm West.

State Affair

Back in the early Seventies at the beginning of my music career, I remember seeing lots of adverts and reviews in the Oxford Mail for a show band called State Affair. They went on to be an established and very well received group not only in Oxfordshire but all over the south of England with a history of just over 20 years. This is not the only reason they are in the book, I remember them being at the centre of a voting scandal in a television talent show in 1978 that enraged a huge amount of people in Oxford!

Bassist Pete Myatt takes up the story.

'The name State Affair was thought up by a friend of mine with whom I went to school with at Fitzharrys in Abingdon in 1967. We started a band in the fourth year, as did a lot of young people at the time, and this lasted a few years, then we all went our separate ways. My next musical move was to get a job with a group called the Treble Tones. They were Mick Harris (vocals), Pete Horwood (sax) and Rex Hastings drums). After I joined they decided to call themselves Treble Tones Plus One. This was October 1971 and we played for a couple of years at a variety of venues until 1973. Our drummer became ill and stopped playing so we looked around for a stand-in. We knew of Mick Harris (mentioned earlier in the book playing for The Electrons at the Town Hall) so we asked him to stand in and he agreed. The gig was at Cowley Conservative Club and we went down really well. Mick's style really suited the group so we asked him to join full time. He said yes and in October 1973 we changed the name to State Affair.'

Courtesy of Oxford Mail /Oxford Times
(Newsquest Oxford)

Now it must have been interesting having two Mick Harrises in the same band, one on vocals, one on drums, and to complicate matters even more the lads used to play quite often at the British Legion and the social secretary there was, yes you've guessed it, Mick Harris! This must have been interesting when the cry went up 'whose round is it next?' Anyway back to Pete…

'We spent the next couple of years getting a name for ourselves, playing all the British Legions and Conservative and Labour clubs. We also appeared quite often at Morris Motors Social Club and Pressed Steel Club, Roman Way. These were always great places to play. State Affair also expanded their horizons and played American bases at Upper Heyford, Fairford, Mildenhall, Croughton and Lakenheath, where we always enjoyed the nights and so did the airmen and women.'

In 1976 there was a TV talent show called New Faces and one week three girl vocalists called the 'M Three' won the postal vote. The name came from the first names of the girls: Maureen, Mary and Marilyn. As Pete recalled: 'Their harmonies were fantastic and we got to know them through our manager, John Dixon, who was related to one of them. He suggested that they should join the group so we invited them to sing with us one night. They went down extremely well and joined us on a permanent basis. This is when State Affair became a proper show band.'

In the same year, State Affair applied for an audition for Opportunity Knocks, another high-profile talent contest on BBC 1 hosted by a gentleman by the name of Hughie Green. State Affair passed the audition with flying colours but unfortunately scheduling mistakes meant they did not appear on the television that year. The following year they received an invitation to audition for the show again in Southampton. They were down to two girls, as Mary had gone on to sing opera.

Pete said: 'The audition was at 9.30 in the morning and the girls were like a breath of fresh air, laughing and giggling. Hughie really liked us; he was tapping his pipe on the piano and singing along. He said he wanted us to appear on his show. A few months later we got a call to say we were going on 6 February 1978.'

State Affair won on their first week both in the studio on the 'clapometer' a legendary device that was supposed to measure the volume of the applause. But more importantly, they won the postal vote. The postal ballot was the important vote (no telephone vote technology or email in those days!). Thousands of people voted for State Affair, but unfortunately they used second class stamps so the votes didn't get their on time.

Pete added: 'The wife of the producer ran a talent school and one of the acts came

from there so she got all of the pupils to vote for that act. One of the mothers rang Opportunity Knocks and told them what had been happening and it was then decided that we should have won the contest but three weeks later the contest was shelved due to contractual matters, so we never got to go back on the All Winners Final!'

As we say in show business, there is no such thing as bad publicity, and on the back of this scandal, which was covered at the time in the Oxford Mail, the bookings came flooding in.

Pete at this point said that he needed to tip his hat to The Education, another showband in Oxford at the time. He said: 'After years of living in their shadow we were suddenly headline.'

After various line-up changes during the following years, State Affair finally played their last gig in Northampton as a three piece, a very low key exit for a band that entertained Oxfordshire and beyond for the best part of 20 years. I'm sure there are many people in Oxford who remember them and danced to them with their future spouses. I saw them once and they were a great show band!

Steamroller

Robert in action.

Courtesy of Oxford Mail /Oxford Times (Newsquest Oxford)

I had been playing for a few years when the Corn Dolly opened and the young Hayward decided to check it out.

Walking down the stairs one Saturday night I was hit in the rib cage by the sound of the wonderful juggernaut of a band called Steamroller. Pausing briefly to buy a can of Colt 45 (well it was the Seventies) I stood there blown away by the power and talent of this band. They didn't reach the heady heights of national distinction but no book about the Sixties and Seventies music in Oxford would be complete without them. This was the band that pushed the boundaries and the one everyone aspired to be like. I, like many others, thought they were great.

Formed in 1970 by guitarist Robert Wakeley, Steamroller was originally a four-piece rhythm and blues unit. I have mentioned Robert earlier in the book when he played with Mal Ryder and the Spirits. Mal is quoted as saying 'Robert is the best guitarist he had seen' a statement with which I and a lot of others agree.

I was lucky enough to catch up with Bob at the music box shop on the Cowley Road owned by another Oxford music legend, Larry Reddington.

He recalled: 'At the start I had Pete Cox on vocals and guitar Roger Warner on bass and Dick Stone on drums. We were signed to the Trevor Benham Agency and soon found ourselves playing gigs all over the south of England in pubs and clubs.'

After a while Dick and Peter left and Robert decided to make Steamroller a three-piece and replaced Dick with his good friend Larry Reddington on drums. Apart from a brief period as a duo, this was the format the group stuck with. This line-up stayed together for around three years until Larry went off to join Prism, another popular and well loved Oxford Band. The line-up changed again and in came Steve Winston for a short while and they played a few local gigs at Whites Bar and the newly opened Corn Dolly.

Robert told me: 'After Steve left Roger and myself played as a duo for a while until one day Roger said that he knew a drummer called John Martyr and thought we should try him out. He came along one night when were playing the Corn Dolly got on his kit and was fantastic; he was in straight away!"

This was the classic line-up that I remember, they were great band and Rob is right, John was, and still is a bit special. (We drummers don't normally praise other drummers – it's just one of those things!)

During the following four years the boys were regulars at the Dolly, to the extent that they kept their equipment there.

Robert insisted that I mention another member of the group.

'Howard Barrett was our road manager and sound engineer and was just as important to the band than any of the musicians.'

I remember Howard as a wizard of the mixing desk and think his knowledge gave Steamroller the edge over other local bands. He left the band eventually and turned professional which proved very successful. As this book goes to print Howard is drum technician with Simply Red.

John behind the Skins (drums).

Roger, very heavy!!

Courtesy of Oxford Mail / Oxford Times (Newsquest Oxford)

At this time when the lads had a residency at the pub, the Corn Dolly became part of the national gig circuit and many good local and-up-and coming national bands played there but Steamroller were the yardstick by which they were measured. They were – and still are – all good at their trade but anyone who witnessed the main man Robert's spine-tingling opening notes on Purple Haze knows there is only one other person that can make it sound that good and that's the man who wrote it!

Eventually in early 1976 John decided to turn pro, so left the band, ending up in another local band called Mr Big (see local heroes) who had a national hit with Romeo. He was replaced by another very good local drummer (crikey two drum compliments in one story – I must be getting soft!) called Mark Freeman. He stayed until the end of 1976 when the group disbanded.

For a year there followed the Robert Wakeley Band, this was a classic example of a good group at the wrong time. New Wave was in and blues and rock was out. Disillusioned, the band folded.

Robert reformed Steamroller early in 1978 with another drummer, Les Postlewaite, and continued until 31 December 1978 when they played their last gig at the Corn Dolly. After this Robert gave his beloved guitar away to the then road manager Mick Hutton and didn't played again ... until May 2009, when Robert, Roger and Larry reformed for a charity gig at the Regal, Cowley Road, which was a triumph.

They still look good and sound great. Long may they continue, the Mighty Steamroller.

Mal Ryder

Born on February 27, 1944 in Llanfrechfa, Wales, Mal (real name Paul Colling) moved to Oxford when he was 2½ years old and went to school in Wolvercote until he was 15. On leaving school he got a job at the Southern Electricity Board. Like many others of his age in the city, he started going to dances in the evenings to meet girls.

Mal told me: 'I made friends with a group of semi-professional musicians called The Meteors. One day at a wedding at which they were playing I was egged on by my

Mal, left, and the band in Oxford.

MAL RYDER and THE SPIRITS

workmates to sing a song with the group as I was always singing at work. I chose the Gene Vincent song Say Mama but they played a joke on me by giving me the wrong key. Luckily we were all a bit drunk so nobody really noticed.'

The Meteors were impressed and asked Mal along to a rehearsal. It went well and they invited him to join the band. They played around Oxford in the clubs and pubs and also the American bases.

After the Meteors, Mal joined another local band called the Spirits, their vocalist Pete Cox, having been called up. He went professional (having been sacked by the SEB for not attending night school) and the Spirits moved north to Doncaster where there were plenty of gigs in the working men's clubs. They issued their first single in 1967 called Cry Baby. On a trip to London's Battersea Fun Fair where lots of groups went to promote their records they were signing autographs to the accompanyment of the backing band: the Rolling Stones!

'Like many English bands at the time we went over to Germany to a place called Vilenhagen and played in a club called the Big Ben. On a second trip we played in Cologne, Frankfurt and Duisburg. We played for a while but eventually the group broke up. The stress of playing six hours a day, five days a week being too much for some. We moved back to Oxford and I started working with my dad as a bricklayer.'

In 1965, Mal joined a band called the Primitives, another semi-pro Oxford band who asked him to sing with them. The Primitives moved to Northampton and acquired some new managers, Cyd and Mayer Cipin (owners of the cinema where they rehearsed) and Les Jaffa.

In January 1966, they went on a month's tour of Norway and went down a storm. Mal told me: 'It seemed as though they'd never seen anything like us, we felt like the Beatles.' The band also had a contract to tour Europe. First a month and a half in Montpelier, France, then to the Piper Club in Viareggo, Italy. The Italians fell in love with the band, then called Mal Ryder and the Primitives and they stayed for a few years, releasing quite a few hit singles.

Mal eventually went solo and stayed in Italy, where he lives today. He is still a huge star in Italy, appearing on TV and performing live. Mal told me that over the years he has sold more than 10 million records, not bad for a rejected SEB apprentice!

The Spirits, a young Bob Wakley on the left.

Mr Big

Courtesy of Oxford Mail /Oxford Times (Newsquest Oxford)

By the mid-Seventies, Oxford had become something of a backwater in terms of the national music scene. Then, in early 1977, almost out of the blue a local band rose to the heady heights of No 4 in the charts. It was Mr Big with Romeo. Most of us in Oxford went out and bought it (support your local band), but we were far from alone as, at its peak, it sold 100,000 copies a week.

I caught up with founder member Jeff Pain (aka Dicken) and asked him how it all started. 'In the late Fifties, my father took me to the London Palladium to see Tommy Steele,' he said. 'We didn't have a lot of money and I remember him selling his watch at a jewellers in Piccadilly to raise enough cash for the tickets. I was so impressed by Tommy I couldn't wait to get home and play the new acoustic guitar my Mum had bought me for Christmas.'

There was a slight problem in that it was a right-handed guitar and Jeff was left-handed. In those days they didn't realise you could get left-handed guitars but Jeff was determined to be a star like Tommy Steele and learned to play right-handed.

In 1967, Oxford-born Jeff formed a band with his school friend Vince Chaulk, called Chaulkie's Painful Leg. Like most young bands, they played cover versions at village halls. But after unsuccessfully taking a demo to Abbey Road studios in London, the band folded.

'In 1969, I became friends with Pete Crowther and we formed Burnt Oak, who played extensively in London,' recalled Jeff. 'Three years later, we changed our name to Mr Big, inspired by a tabloid headline of the day. Our first gig under the new name was at the famous Marquee club.'

Mr Big were signed by Epic Records in 1974 and three singles followed. They were marketed as a Cockney band, pearly suits and all! They often appeared on TV, one of their first slots being in a club in the police drama Softly Softly Taskforce. The programme controller at the time, Muriel Young, was a fan. (Those of you of a certain age will remember Muriel as a friend of Pussy Cat Willum!)

By now the group were regulars at the Marquee and also at London's Speakeasy Club. It was there that they were spotted by Stan Tippins, tour manager for Mott the Hoople. Tippins introduced them to Hoople's manager Bob Hirschman, who added them to his stable.

At the same time Mr Big were recruited by EMI Records and set about recording their first album with producer John Punter. Sweet Silence was released in November 1975 to much acclaim from the music press.

Dicken recalled that month being a particularly good one for the band. He said: 'We were support band to Queen on their Night at the Opera tour around the UK. The good thing about Queen was that they were very fatherly and professional. We were playing through their PA and were never allowed to feel second best. We travelled on the same coach and did about 40 gigs, culminating in with shows at Hammersmith Odeon. Freddie (Mercury) was a lovely man and once bought me a bottle of champagne when he found out it was my birthday. I was celebrating at a restaurant in London and he walked in with Barbara Windsor.'

In 1976, the band added guitarist Eddy Carter to the line-up and after a short tour of Europe supporting Sweet, they embarked on a nationwide tour of their own. They also started work on their second album, for which Romeo was written.

The single was an immediate hit even though Mary Whitehouse managed to have it banned by the BBC for two weeks. Apparently the lyric 'Step back inside me, Romeo' shocked the fabled campaigner. What did she think it meant?

The following year, with the emergence of Punk and New Wave, Mr Big, like many bands at the time, felt they no longer fitted in and broke up.

Dicken and Crowther formed another band called Broken Home, who were well received in mainland Europe and Scandinavia.

Dicken has just re-recorded Romeo and, as this book was going to print, was waiting for the final mix. Let's hope it is another great Oxford success story.

Adrian Hopkins

While never claiming to be a musician, Adrian Hopkins has nevertheless been a huge influence in entertainment both in Oxford and, later, nationally. Quite literally this man has been there, done that, and still sells the tee-shirts!

Oxford born and bred, he still lives in the City. I caught up with him and asked him how it all started.

'I used to go and see bands in the Sixties and really enjoyed it. I went to see Mal Ryder and The Spirits at the Britannia pub in Headington, and somehow at a very young age I ended up on the door taking money for the show. I had left school at 15 and was then doing a toolmakers apprenticeship at Pressed Steel, and I thought this might be a good way to supplement my income, if not with Mal, then maybe other bands.'

At the start of his career, he was a footballer for Rose Hill and then Oxford United. Adrian wanted to be a professional footballer. He also saw the Falling Leaves, who were in the year below him at East Oxford School, in the early Sixties. He knew they played at the Forum and that they were drawing in more people than the jazz bands that used to play there. He thought they were fantastic.

'I went to see them and as friends I asked how much they would get for the Forum gig. They said the Leaves got £5 every Wednesday and I said I could double that for them if they let me be their manager and that's exactly what happened.'

The real kick-start to Adrian's career as a promoter came when he was social secretary for Rose Hill football team. He used to run all their functions at the Community Centre to raise money for the youth team and he became very adept at doing so. It occurred to him that this might be a way of making money for himself as the £3 a week as a toolmaker was not exactly luxury, and anyway Adrian confessed to me that he was probably one of the worst toolmakers at Pressed Steel!

Adrian's biggest coup in his early career was when he spotted an advert for Beatles tickets when they were playing in Birmingham. He drew all his money out of the Post Office, travelled to Britain's second city, queued up and bought 300 tickets. These at the time were like gold dust, the price five shillings (25p).

'I returned to Oxford, went straight to the Oxford Mail and placed an advert and told them I had some Beatles tickets and could provide transport for the Oxford public. Needless to say they put his story on the front page. In the next few days I had queues of people outside my house in Magdalen Road. Some just wanted the tickets so I had to explain to them I didn't work like that, you had to take the coach.'

This established Adrian as the top local promoter.

Adrian continued to promote bands and manage The Falling Leaves and then in March 1964 he received a very important phone call.

'I had just arrived home and was having my tea when I got a call from a gentleman called Arthur Howse. He was a top national promoter in the Sixties and that night he was presenting a package of acts at the New Theatre consisting of Cilla Black, Billy J. Kramer and the Dakotas, and Gene Pitney from the USA. Arthur informed me that Cilla Black had been taken ill and that her doctor had said she could not play Oxford that night.'

Pausing a few minutes to finish his tea, Adrian roared round Oxford on his motorbike to tell everyone in The Falling Leaves and within two hours of the phone call they were on stage.

When it was announced to the audience that Cilla couldn't perform that night there was quite a lot of booing but when we told them that the local lads had taken her place the crowd erupted into cheers. At the end of the show Gene Pitney was so impressed with the Oxford band that he said that next time he appeared in the city he wanted them to support him and true to his word, they did.

In 1965 Adrian opened a club at the Bridge Hotel in the Oxfordshire village of Wheatley. At the time he was still attempting to be a toolmaker and was also doing discos at night, they were called Hopeless Hoppy's Mobile Discos. It was when he was doing a gig at the Bridge that he thought the back room might be a good place to showcase groups. On the opening night at the newly named Garden of Eden club the headliners were the Applejacks, whose single Have I the Right was in the national charts at the time, and as a bit of insurance, Oxford's own Falling Leaves.

Over the following months many acts appeared at the Garden of Eden that were to go on to great things, including Elton John with Steampacket, Rod Stewart, and a group from Birmingham called Listen, whose singer was a young man called Robert Plant.

Everyone old enough can remember the late Sixties with its peace and love movement that culminated in 1969 with the festival at Woodstock in the USA. Well, you might

Oscar Peterson.

Adrian and Anne Hopkins with Johnny Cash.

Adrian with
Ella Fitzgerald.

be surprised to know that Oxfordshire pre-empted this by two years. In 1967 Adrian promoted the first ever concert at Blenheim Palace, Woodstock.

"I was asked to promote a concert at the Palace for the benefit of the St John Ambulance,' he said. 'The gig was on a stage directly in front of the main entrance. On the bill were Manfred Mann, P. P. Arnold with her backing group 'The Nice' Jeff Beck with Rod Stewart on vocals Simon Dupree and the Big Sound.'

Everyone has a great afternoon in the sun and the crowd numbered more than 3,000.

After this Adrian's career really took off ,although he was still working at the car factory and still managing the Falling Leaves. He took to promoting groups on the newly formed Chrysalis labels (the name came from a combination of its two founder members Chris Wright and Terry Ellis, something I never knew until Adrian told me. How obvious it seems now!)

At the ripe old age of 28 Adrian finally went professional, leaving the car factory on a Friday night. He took off his boiler suit and was straight on the bus to Edinburgh with Cat Stevens, who was on the books at Chrysalis along with Jethro Tull, Ten Years After and Procol Harum. In the late Seventies, Adrian also promoted Lindisfarne and Hawkwind.

Later Chrysalis signed a young man called Leo Sayer. This was their first step into the pop music charts and they liked him because he was instantly recognisable on TV and really put the record label in the public eye.

During the following years Adrian went on to promote many legends in the music business including Ella Fitzgerald, Liza Minelli, Jack Jones, Tony Bennett, Tommy Steel, Freddie Starr, and the legendary Johnny Cash.

When he left Chrysalis to go his own way, Adrian was approached by Steeleye Span, a group he had been promoting, to be their manager. He accepted and looked after them for the best part of 20 years.

'During the mid Seventies I heard a young band from Dublin called Thin Lizzy who I decided to promote,' he said. 'Initially things weren't that good but they eventually took their place in the UK's rock hierarchy.'

I was in a band that was playing the Corn Dolly one Saturday and we took ourselves off to Taphouses Music Shop. The mission, to be honest, I can't remember – probably some new strings. While faffing around (see Russell Acott) two tall and rather elegant men came in. They were Phil Lynott and Scott Goram, bass player and lead guitar for Thin

Lizzy appearing that night at the New Theatre. We chatted for quite a while and two nicer people you could not wish to meet, a sentiment echoed by Adrian.

Mr Hopkins also put his weight behind a new Australian band called AC/DC and acquired the merchandising rights for a young Newcastle band called Dire Straits.

So there you have it, Adrian Hopkins, Oxford born and bred, has had involvement with so many UK music acts, it reads like a who's who of the last four decades.

True to his roots Adrian still lives in Oxford and is still very much a part of the UK music scene, promoting James Last, Jethro Tull and a young upstart called Cliff Richards.

I was lucky enough to interview him and his charming wife, Anne, at his home and halfway through needed to use the little boy's room. Now, there aren't many people that have a signed gold disc from Cliff Richards in their downstairs toilet!!

Good luck to you Adrian, a great Oxford entrepreneur!

Roy Young

While researching and interviewing for this book and BBC Oxford, one name kept cropping up more than any other when the Sixties music scene in Oxford was mentioned.

The name is Roy Young, a gentleman whom I and many others consider Oxford's first superstar.

Evacuated from London at the start of the second World War when Roy was five, his family came to Oxford. 'One thing I will

Roy, left, and Cliff.

always remember was how different the countryside was to London,' he recalled. 'The smell of the cows, pigs, and sheep. I was so intrigued that on Wednesdays, cattle market day at the Oxpens, I would help the farmers load the beasts in and out of the trucks. When I returned home my mum would throw me in the bath, I smelt so bad!'

On arriving in Oxford, the family had to sleep in the old Majestic cinema along the Botley Road where MFI used to be. Eventually they moved to a house on Blackfriars Road in St Ebbes, where Roy spent most of his youth.

Roy started playing piano at the age of eight. There was always a piano in the house as his mother was a pianist and played in various pubs in Oxford. She had a unique style because she only played the black notes. The audiences loved her, and young Roy (no pun intended) would listen outside (no children allowed in pubs in those days) and decided he would like to play in front of an audience.

Roy reminisced with me.

'My first school was Poplar School in Cowley, where the original press steel car factory was, but I later moved to South Oxford School in St Aldates closer to where I lived.

'At the age of 10 I was introduced to Boogie Woogie style of playing piano by listening to Pete Johnson, Albert Ammons, and Meade Lux Lewis on records and my mum playing pub songs. I used to look forward to going home after school to play the piano because I knew all the kids on my street would be gathering around my window waiting for me to play. I guess you would call that my first gig.'

Roy's first professional performance was at the Carpenters Arms on Between Towns Road in Cowley. Word got around that Mrs Young's son was playing there and the pub got so packed that Roy used to perform in a large hall at the back of the pub. With so much popularity it wasn't long before he was gigging at the Town Hall and New Theatre.

It was at this time that Roy's life turned a decisive corner in his musical career.

'One day a mate came home after travelling around the world in the Merchant Navy,' he said. 'He was tanned, happy and had lots of money and I was very envious. As I wanted to stand on my own two feet I decided to enlist.

While travelling on board I performed many shows for the crew and passengers with pianist Russ Conway, who later got into the music business himself with his first No.1 hit Sidesaddle.'

Roy visited Australia with the Merchant Navy and found himself at a loose end wandering around Sydney.

'I walked by a cinema that was featuring a film called The Blackboard Jungle and decided to spend a couple of hours watching it, unaware that this movie was about to turn my life around. The opening song was Rock Around The Clock by Bill Haley and The Comets. This was in the days before rock n roll and it just blew me away. I went through the entire film waiting for the next showing so that I could hear it again! The manager of the cinema told me that if I wanted to stay in the cinema I had to pay again!', so I did.

On returning to England Roy embraced this new form of music and felt confident enough to become professional.

He told me of the time. 'I decided to approach the agencies in London. It was harder to get into rock 'n' roll than I thought. I spent at least two or three months walking around London visiting different agencies with no luck. The money I had saved was running out. I'll always remember walking around the streets with a loaf of bread under my arm, that's all I could afford.'

Determined to break through, Roy carried on and found himself outside a hairdressing salon and a sign saying, 'Carna Variety Agency', 4th floor. Being so tired he decided not to bother but 1/2 mile down the road the thought 'what if' crossed his mind and he went back.

'I walked into the office, a slightly dishevelled figure and the receptionist asked me what I wanted. I said, my name is Roy Young, I'm a rock 'n roll singer and piano player and I want to be a pro. Out came one of the greatest guys in my life - Jack Falon. We talked and

To
Trevor
Thanks a million
best of luck
Roy Young's +
The Beatles
Star Club
Hamburg
1962

he gave me five pounds and said go and get washed up and have something to eat. Be back here by seven and I'll have a contract ready for you. You'll be doing a show tonight with Johnny Duncan and the Bluegrass Boys who at that time were a huge skiffle band. Your name is now Roy Rock'em Young.

'I was shocked and surprised at the speed this happened but I later found out that he had turned down a young man called Tommy Steele a couple of months previously who went on to have a UK No.1, Rock With the Caveman.'

Later Roy auditioned for a new pop show Oh Boy, the early Sixties version of Top of the Pops. Roy ran his fingers along the old piano and launched into a raucous version of the rock and roll classic Long Tall Sally. Jack Good, the show's producer, grabbed him and shouted 'You're in, you're in.' Jack loved little Richard and Roy certainly fitted the bill. Roy went on to do a number of TV programmes for Jack and also the BBC series Drumbeat. It was at this time that Roy became known as 'England's Little Richard'.

After touring extensively with Cliff Richard, Roy met Reg Calvert in Rugby. Reg told Roy about the music scene in Hamburg and booked him into the 'Top 10' club on the Reeperbahn for three weeks. The shows were so successful that he was offered a lifetime contract. He played there for the next three months and then came back to England for a break. On Roy's return to the club, two young men from Liverpool rushed up to greet him as he was getting out of his taxi. They were Paul McCartney and John Lennon from an unknown group called the Beatles. They had seen Roy on TV and were big fans.

Roy was to meet the Liverpool band again in 1962, when he received the first contract to appear at the Star-Club, originally a cinema, in the Grosser Freiheit, Hamburg.

'Manfred Weissleder, the owner of the cinema (the Stern Kino), called me to his office and told me he was making plans to launch the most famous rock 'n' roll club in the world.'

He certainly did that! He offered Roy a three-year contract with amazing money and a brand new car which he agreed to sign. It was at the Star-Club that The Beatles enlisted Roy to play keyboard and sing back-up vocals with them. At that time, Beatles manager Brian Epstein approached Roy with an offer to return to England to procure an international record contract with the band. It was this record that ultimately thrust The Beatles into international superstardom. Unfortunately, Roy was in the middle of a three-year exclusive contract with the Star-Club and regretfully turned down the offer. Roy knew he was turning down an offer to join a band that had something special.

During his time at the Star-Club Roy played with some of the great rock and roll artists

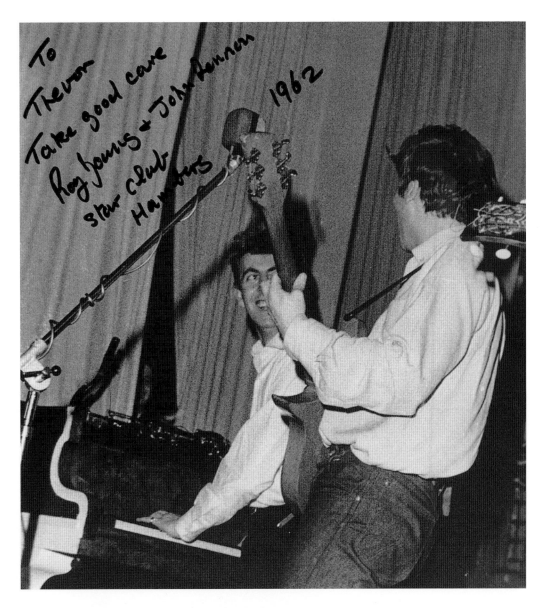

To
Thevor
Take good care
Roy Young + John Bennon
star club
Hambers
1962

such as Little Richard, Chuck Berry, Ray Charles and The Beatles.

In 1964, after his contract with the Star-Club expired, Roy returned to England and joined Cliff Bennett and the Rebel Rousers, who were managed by Epstein. As well as doing many other shows with The Beatles in London, Roy joined them on their 1966 tour of Germany and later worked with the band to produce a version of Got to Get You Into My Life, on which Paul McCartney joined him on keyboards.

When Cliff Bennett left the band Roy took over and toured extensively around England. It was during this time he met agent/manager Laurie O'Leary. In 1969 he booked the

To
Trevor
great to see you again
lots of luck
Roy Young, Paul McCartney,
George Harrison
Star Club
Hamburg
1962

The very special pictures on pages 66–71 were given by Roy Young.

They show Roy playing in Hamburg with The Beatles.

Rebel Rousers on a three-month stint in the Bahamas where Roy met his lovely wife Carol.

When he returned to England, Laurie persuaded Roy to form the Roy Young Band.

The band usually headlined one-off gigs. He played the Speakeasy in London which his manager also managed. It was a well known club that many international stars frequented often after their own shows.

While touring he found himself on shows with such artists as Sly and the Family Stone, Sweet, Mungo Gerry, Black Sabbath, Fleetwood Mac, Family etc. Roy toured with Deep Purple in Germany and Chuck Berry throughout England where he recorded the live hit for Chuck, My Ding-a-ling, which reached No.1 in the British charts.

'In 1976 I received a call at my home in Oxford. It was David Bowie. He wanted me to join him in Los Angeles to record on his next album. He wanted to start recording the following week. I tried to get a quick visa but this proved impossible so I didn't go. A year later to the day I received a phone call at the Speakeasy Club in London where I was appearing. It was David asking me to join him on his latest album 'Low' that he was to record in Berlin, although eventually he did it at La Chateau studio in Paris. This time I could go.

'David is very well educated and extremely organised with his music. He knew exactly where he was going and what he wanted. I hit it off very well with him and we became good friends. He is a true Little Richard fan and was inspired by my voice being known as England's Little Richard.'

In 1977 Roy moved abroad and toured the Roy Young Band extensively throughout Canada and the USA. He also teamed up with the legendary British blues artist Long John Baldry, as well as playing with him; Roy also became his manager for a couple of years.

For the purposes of this book, this is where we leave Roy Young's career.

I do feel, however, that a quick paragraph of what happened next is appropriate, even if it is outside our timeline.

In the Eighties Roy toured with Ian Hunter and Mick Ronson throughout Canada and America, also doing some producing. He also spent several years in Miami appearing with some of his old mates Gerry and the Pacemakers, Peter Noone, Eric Burdon, The Hollies, The Searchers, Manfred Mann and The Troggs.

In 1995 he headlined a Star-Club reunion at the New Theatre in Hamburg and made a personal appearance in Europe with Yoko Ono at John Lennon's Art Show.

In 1996 he played on John Lennon's Steinway piano at a charitable event in Toronto and also recorded some tracks for an album.

In 2002 he made an album in Nashville called Still Young and in 2005 revived the Star Combo to record four songs in Toronto.

Roy moved back to England in 2006.

(Phew I'm out of breath just writing this.)

As this book goes to print in the summer of 2009, Roy has just released a double CD celebrating 50 years as a professional musician, Roy Young…the best of 50 Years.

Keep rocking young Roy, Oxford's first true superstar.

CHAPTER 5
Trev's Trivia

'Legs' Larry Smith, drummer with The Bonzo Dog Do Da Band, was born in Oxford on January 18 1944.

Nik Turner (born Nicholas Turner) was born in Oxford on 28 August 1940. He is best known as co-founder and sax player with space rock group Hawkwind.

The video for Kate Bush's classic hit Cloudbusting featuring Donald Sutherland was shot just outside Oxford on Dragon Hill next to White Horse Hill at Uffington. OK it's not in Oxford but hey, she's gorgeous!

Lonnie Donaghan's 1960 No 1 hit My Old Man's a Dustman was recorded live at the New Theatre in George Street.

Now we all know the Small Faces single Itchycoo Park with its opening line 'Over bridge of sighs, to rest my eyes in shades of green' well this refers to the Bridge of Sighs over Catte Street joining two parts of Hertford College. The group were staying in a hotel in Oxford and spotted a tourist pamphlet in the room describing it.

Clarence Walker, lead singer with the legendary American group, The Drifters, lived in Jericho in his later life. Clarence departed this world in August 2007.

In 1970 Freddie Mercury was singing in a group called Sour Milk Sea. They played two gigs in Oxford, one at the Randolph Hotel and the other on 20 March was a show for the charity Shelter at Highfield Parish Hall in Headington. Shortly after he left the group to join Queen.

2 lovely sights: The Bridge of Sighs and Kate Bush.

The Jeff Beck Group played at Oxford Town Hall on December 23, 1967. On vocals that night was a young man called Rod Stewart.

American Band leader Glenn Miller played one of his last concerts in England at the Churchill Hospital in 1944. The hospital was known at the time as the 91st General and was an American military hospital. It was an open-air concert on the lawn for patients and staff alike. Not long after, on December 15, 1944, Miller boarded an aircraft to fly to Paris and was never seen again.

Local rumour says that Eric Clapton played his first professional gig at the Carfax Assembly Rooms in Oxford in 1965. He had a friend in the city called Ben Palmer and Ben's band was called the Roosters. Now, after a year of research I can tell you that Ben did have a band called the Roosters, he was Eric's friend, and Eric did visit him in 1965, but I still cannot pin down the gig. Still let's keep it in the book because it's great trivia and Eric, if you want to contact me to confirm or deny I would love to hear from you.

One of Oxford's own chart topper Supergrass played their first gig under the name Theodore Super Grass at The Hollybush pub on Osney Island in 1994.

ACKNOWLEDGEMENTS

Over the past few years I have been working freelance for BBC Oxford on the shows 'Inside Lives', The Beatles in Oxford and the Sixties show 'Bringing Back the Good Times'. During this time I have been lucky to interview many people – some members of the audience, some managing and promoting, some playing on stage. Their stories have been fascinating, knowledgeable and fun and I have had the pleasure of broadcasting many of them to the good people of Oxfordshire. All the people I have interviewed have become friends, some very close, and the most enduring memory of all is the delight at telling these stories; their eyes alight, the smile that spreads across their face, and their eagerness to pass on the tale.

To the following (and I hope I haven't missed anyone out) I say a very grateful and humble thank you very much: Elise Alexander, Chris Andrews, Alison Booker, Ron Capel, Nigel Copping, Julian Denson, Simon Edens, Janet Fisher, Diane Gibbs, Joanna Gunhouse, Anastasia Heath, Robert Haynes, Les Hallett, Mick Harris, Adrian Hopkins, Anne Hopkins, Deb and Will Jarvis, Nigel Lawrence, Reg Little, Marcos, Alex and Margaret Messenger, Pete Myatt, Jeff (Dicken) Pain, Alicia Phillips, Mick Phillips, Larry Reddington, Neil Robinson, Mal Ryder, Jeff Samways, gorgeous Marli Santos, Arthur Titherington, Steve Theobald, Robert Wakeley, Roger Warner, Mark Watson, Carol and Roy Young.

Many thanks to the splendid Crispin Jenkinson for writing the introduction to this book and to Alec, Andy, Colleen, Phil, Sarah and all the staff at the Mitre on the High for letting me spend many hours writing there, cuddling a large glass of merlot.

I am indebted to Chris McDowell at the Oxford Mail archives for his help and phenomenal knowledge of his empire.

And finally, a very special thanks to my good friend Sue Elstob and Alan Lees, whose hard work and gentle encouragement made sure I finished this book before the next millennium.

I hope you've enjoyed it. Have fun and keep rocking in Oxford.

Trev

Author photo by Haynes